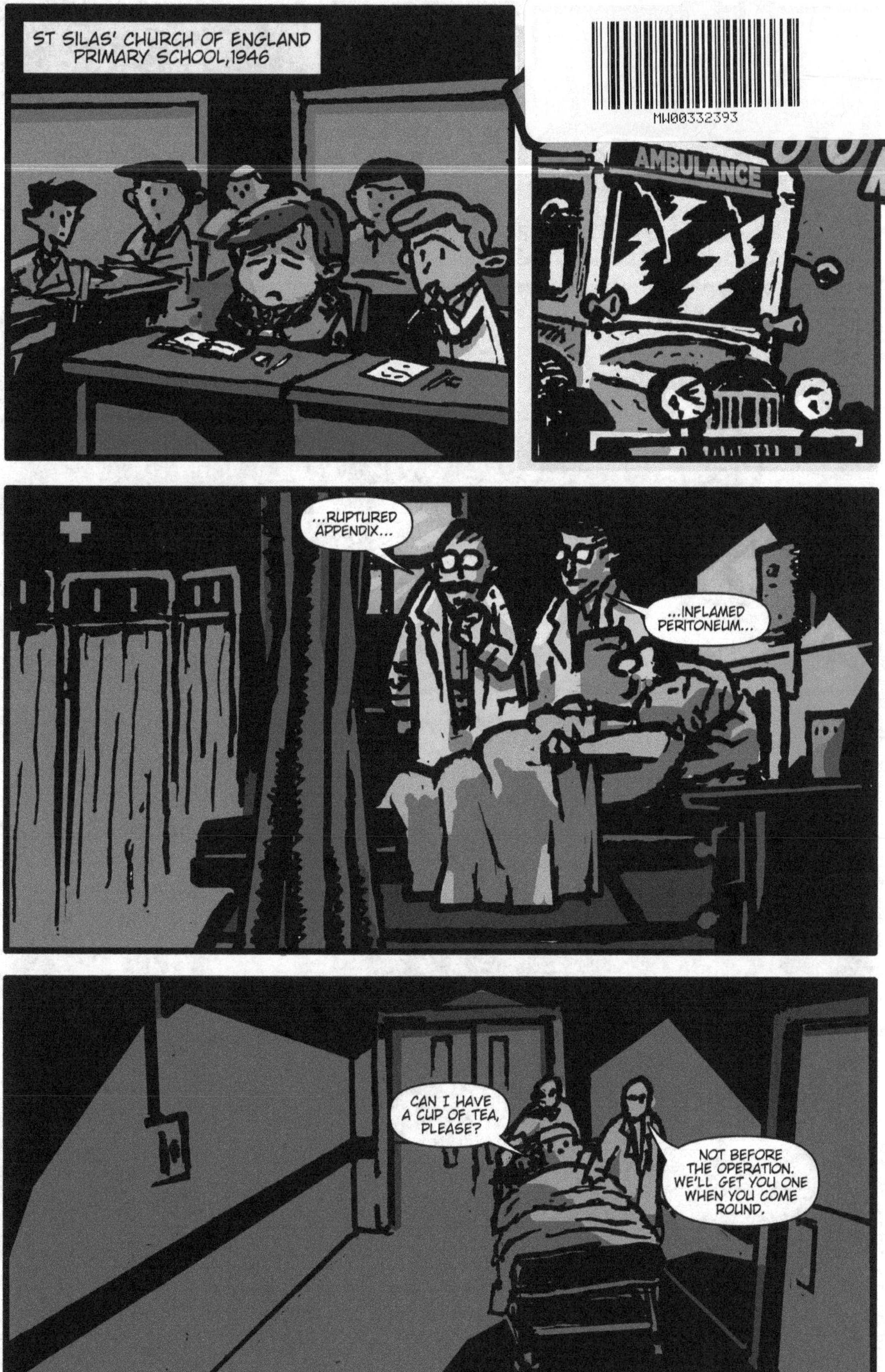

ST SILAS' CHURCH OF ENGLAND PRIMARY SCHOOL, 1946
AMBULANCE
...RUPTURED APPENDIX...
...INFLAMED PERITONEUM...
CAN I HAVE A CUP OF TEA, PLEASE?
NOT BEFORE THE OPERATION. WE'LL GET YOU ONE WHEN YOU COME ROUND.

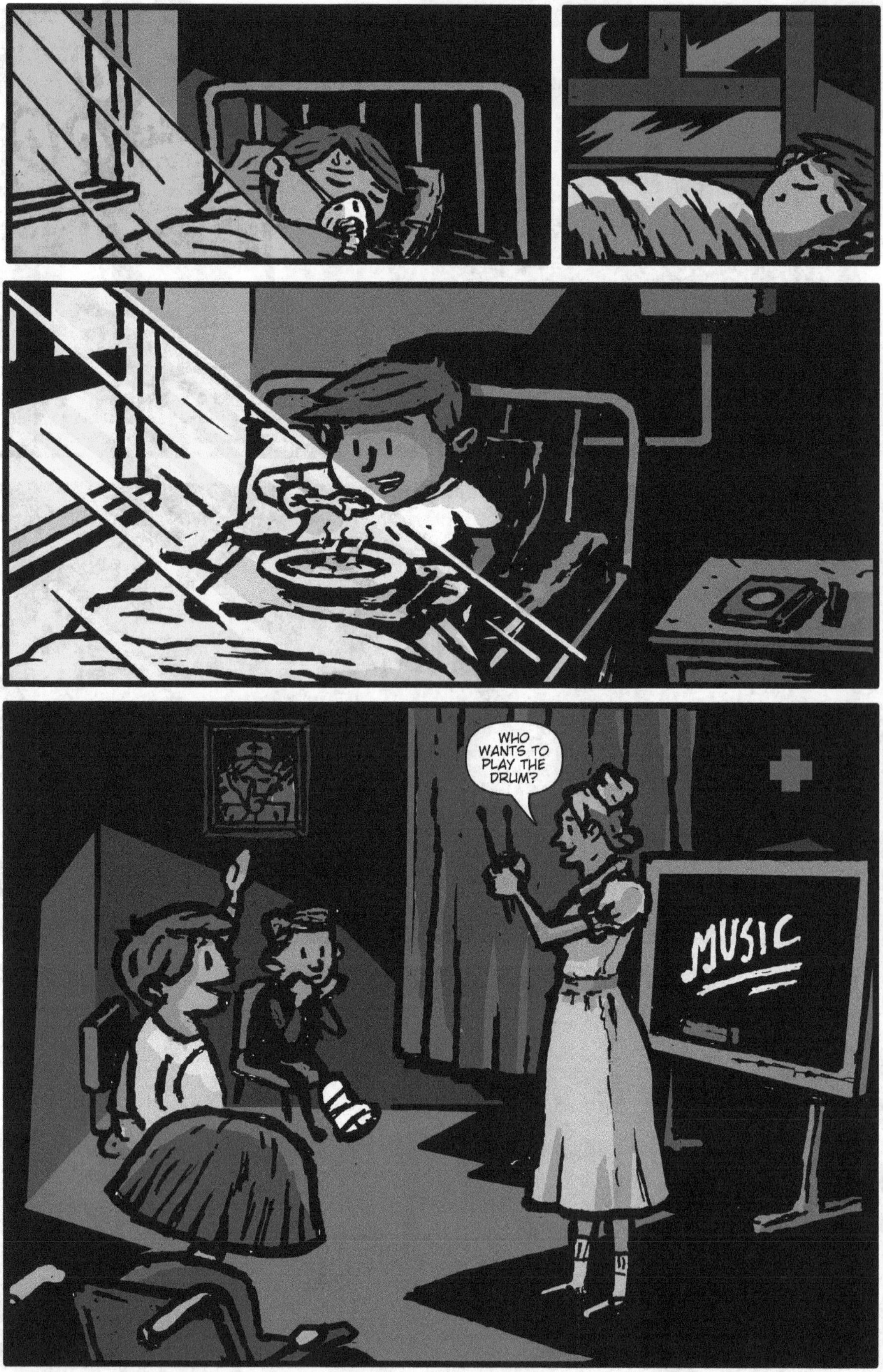
WHO WANTS TO PLAY THE DRUM?
MUSIC

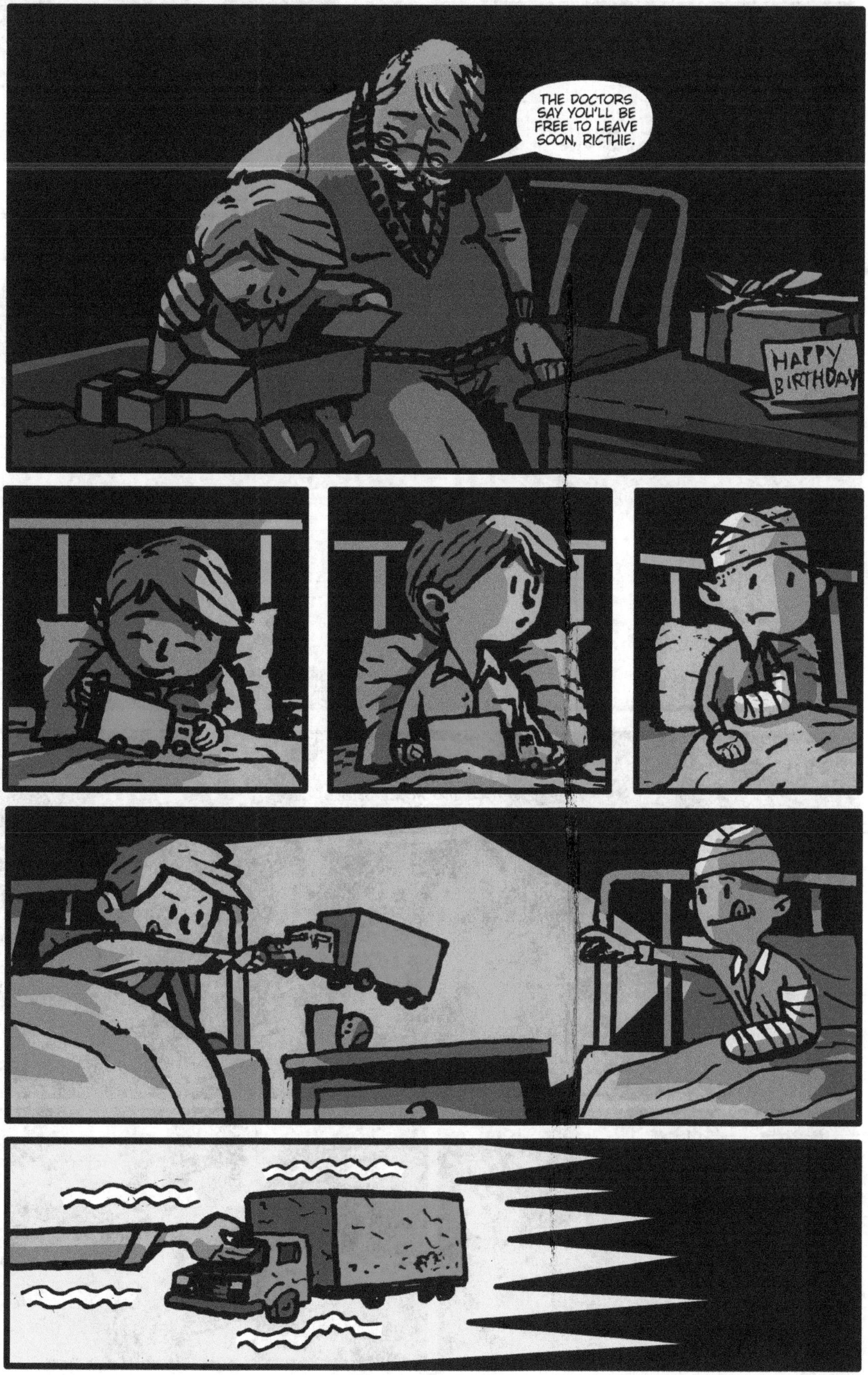
THE DOCTORS SAY YOU'LL BE FREE TO LEAVE SOON, RICTHIE.
HAPPY BIRTHDAY

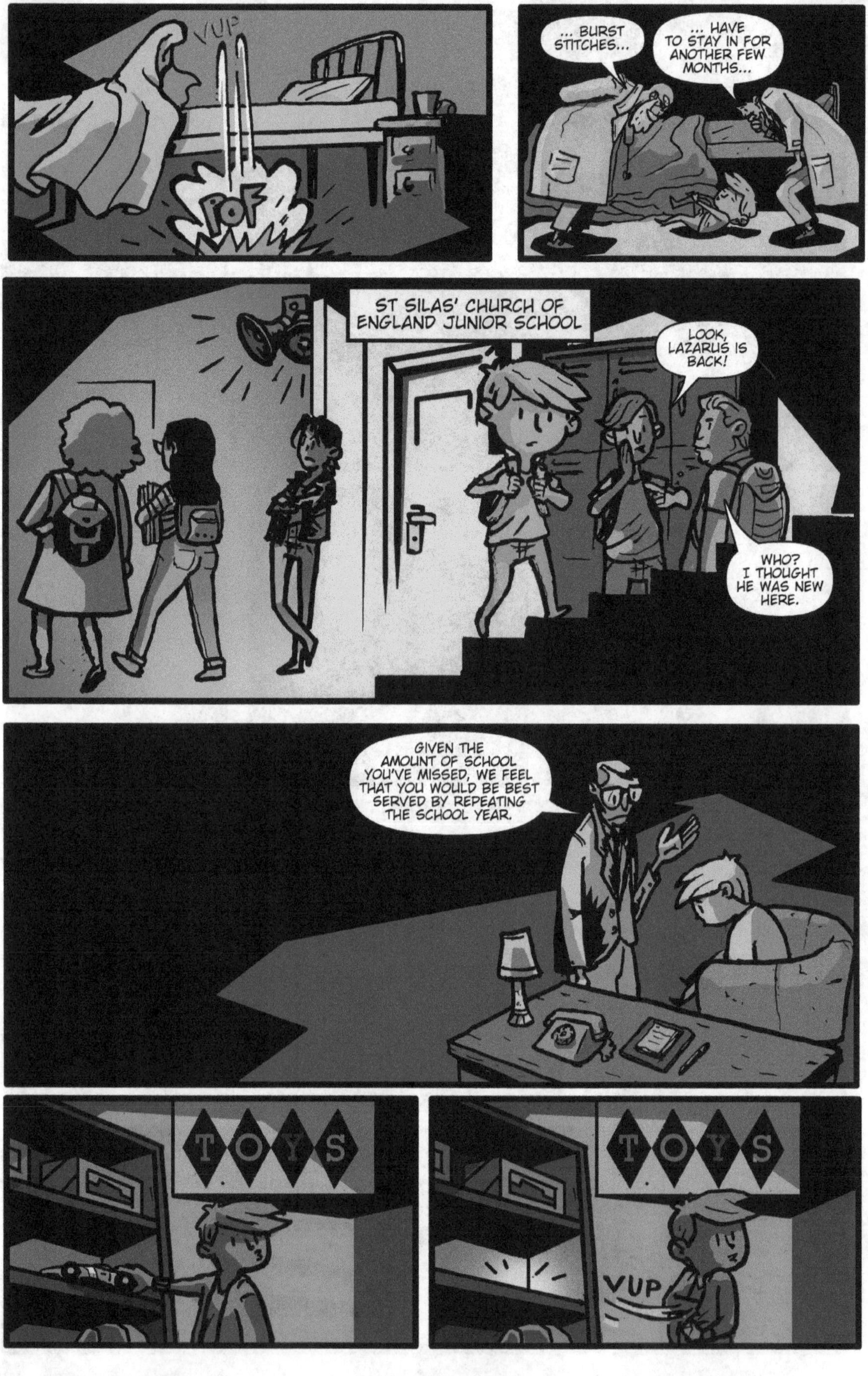
VUP
POF
... BURST STITCHES...
... HAVE TO STAY IN FOR ANOTHER FEW MONTHS...
ST SILAS' CHURCH OF ENGLAND JUNIOR SCHOOL
LOOK, LAZARUS IS BACK!
WHO? I THOUGHT HE WAS NEW HERE.
GIVEN THE AMOUNT OF SCHOOL YOU'VE MISSED, WE FEEL THAT YOU WOULD BE BEST SERVED BY REPEATING THE SCHOOL YEAR.
TOYS
TOYS
VUP

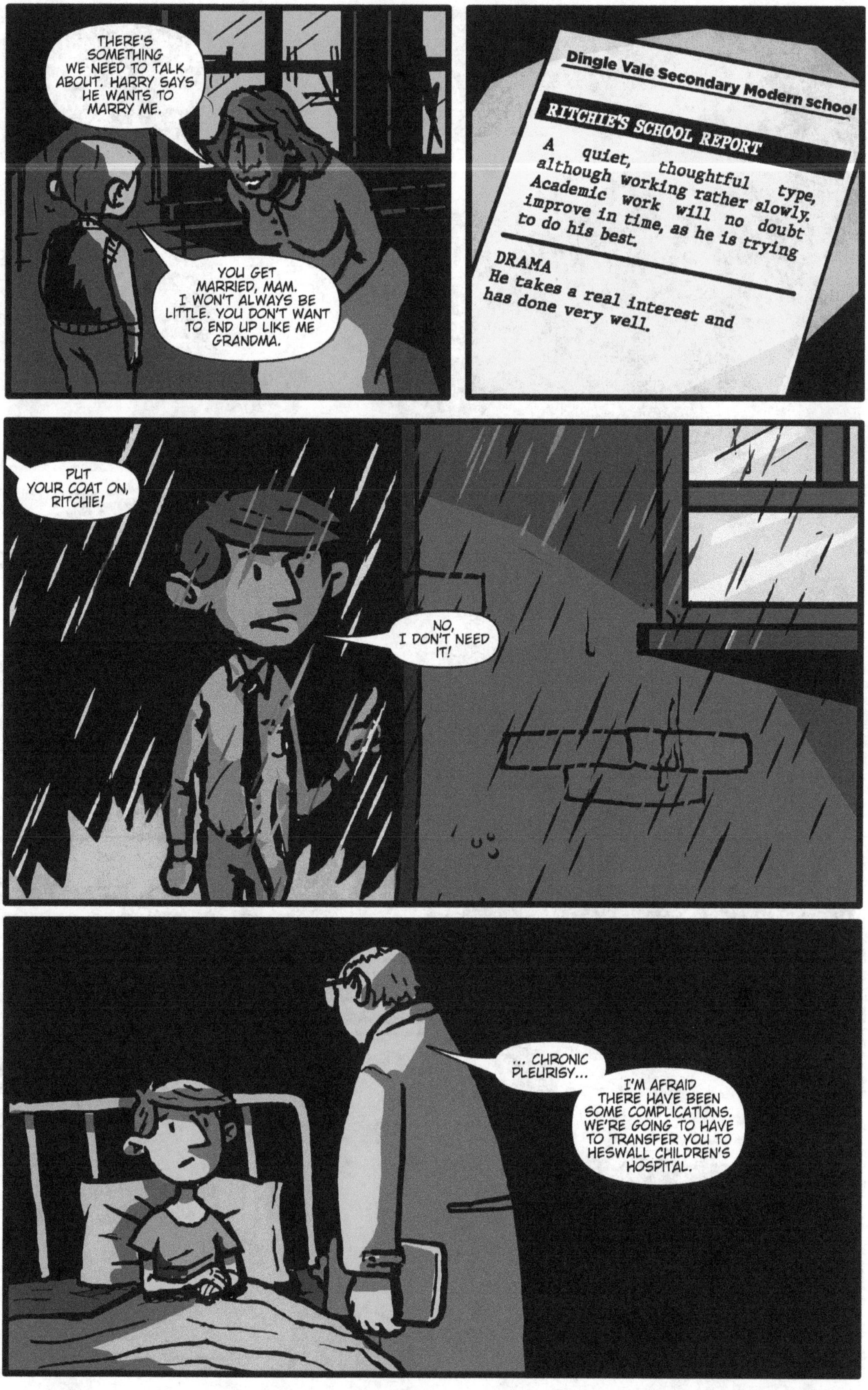
THERE'S SOMETHING WE NEED TO TALK ABOUT. HARRY SAYS HE WANTS TO MARRY ME.
YOU GET MARRIED, MAM. I WON'T ALWAYS BE LITTLE. YOU DON'T WANT TO END UP LIKE ME GRANDMA.
Dingle Vale Secondary Modern school
RITCHIE'S SCHOOL REPORT
A quiet, thoughtful type, although working rather slowly. Academic work will no doubt improve in time, as he is trying to do his best.
DRAMA
He takes a real interest and has done very well.
PUT YOUR COAT ON, RITCHIE!
NO, I DON'T NEED IT!
... CHRONIC PLEURISY...
I'M AFRAID THERE HAVE BEEN SOME COMPLICATIONS. WE'RE GOING TO HAVE TO TRANSFER YOU TO HESWALL CHILDREN'S HOSPITAL.

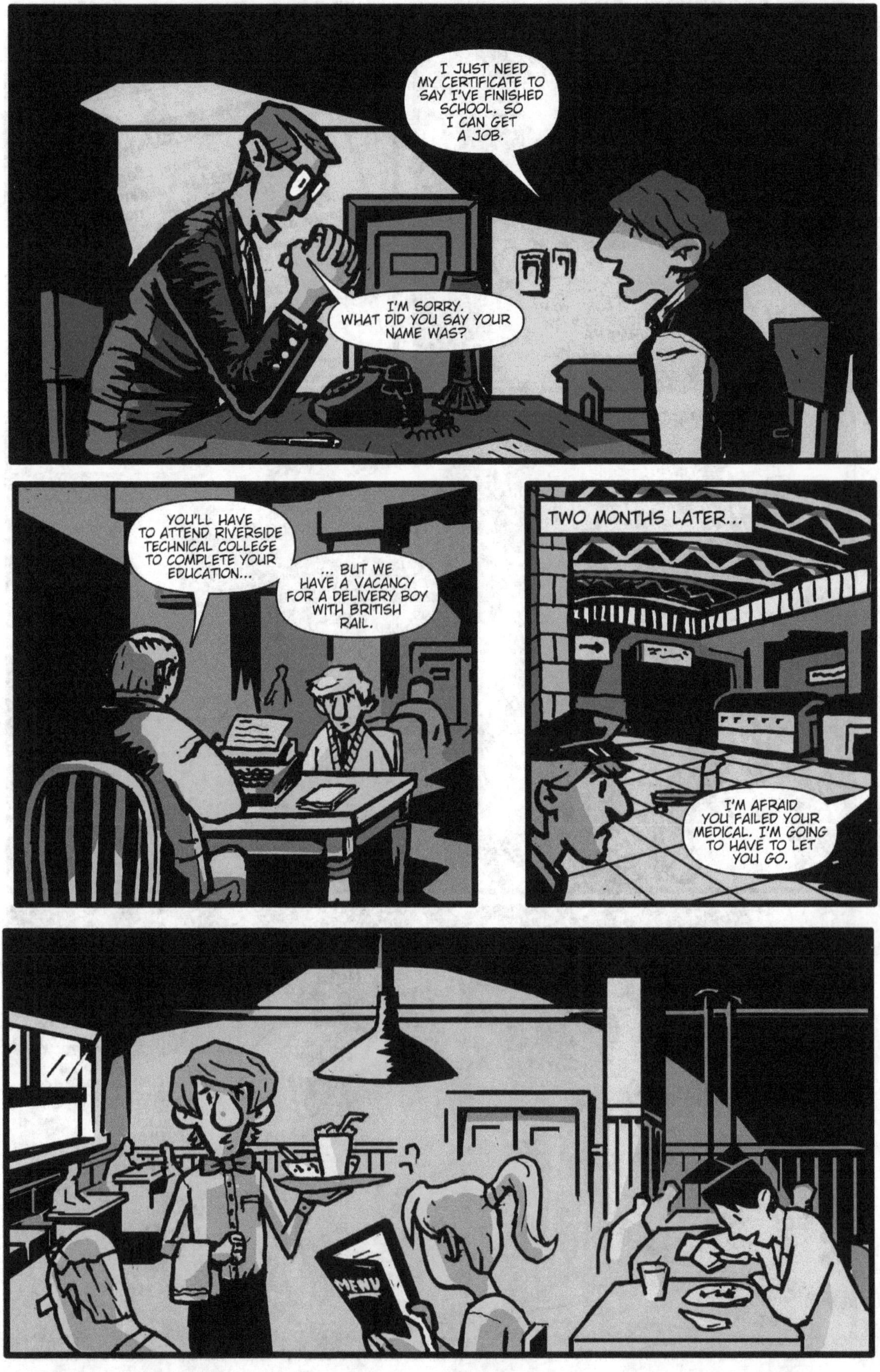

I JUST NEED MY CERTIFICATE TO SAY I'VE FINISHED SCHOOL. SO I CAN GET A JOB.
I'M SORRY. WHAT DID YOU SAY YOUR NAME WAS?
YOU'LL HAVE TO ATTEND RIVERSIDE TECHNICAL COLLEGE TO COMPLETE YOUR EDUCATION...
... BUT WE HAVE A VACANCY FOR A DELIVERY BOY WITH BRITISH RAIL.
TWO MONTHS LATER...
I'M AFRAID YOU FAILED YOUR MEDICAL. I'M GOING TO HAVE TO LET YOU GO.
MENU

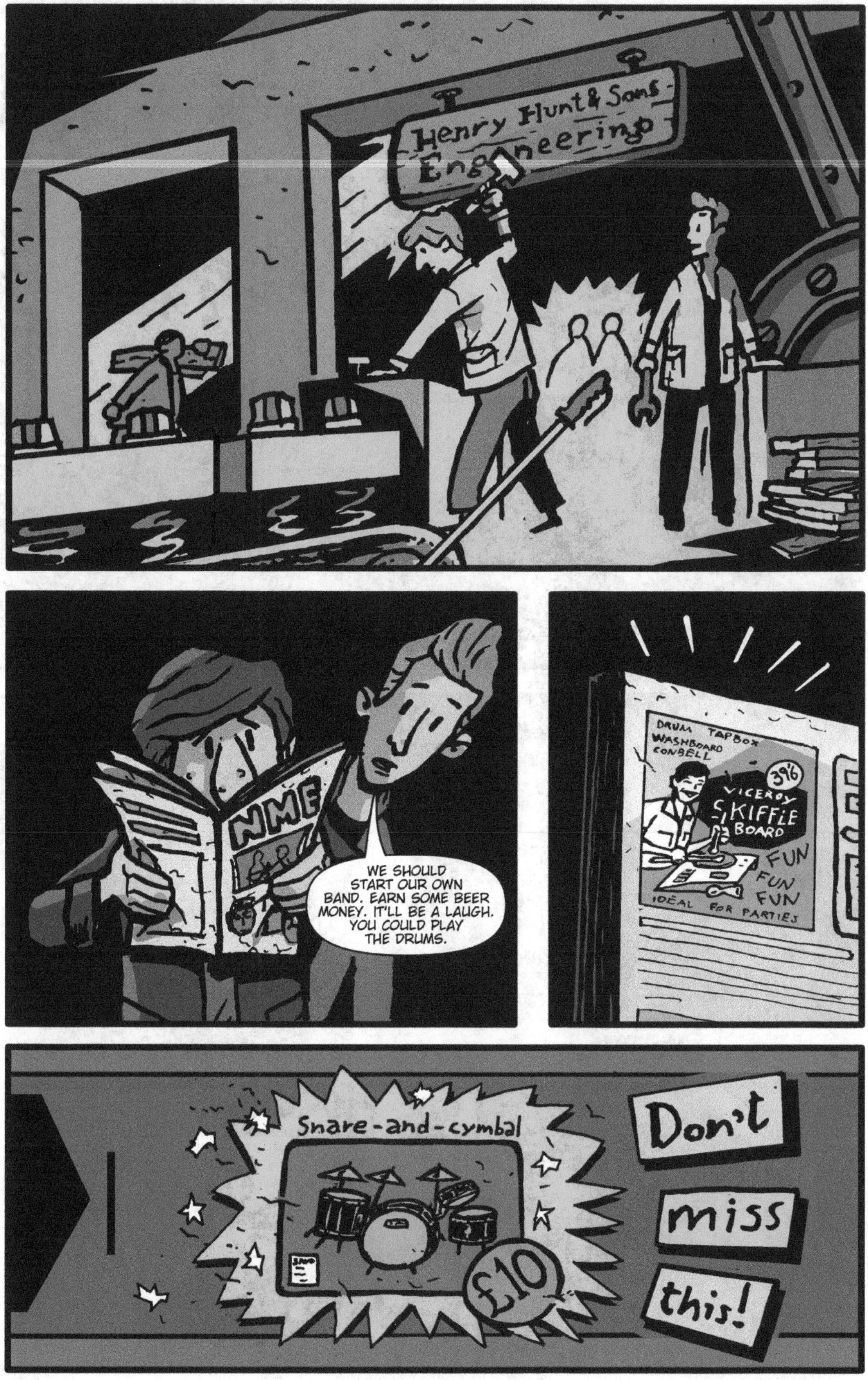
Henry Hunt & Sons
Engineering
NME
WE SHOULD START OUR OWN BAND. EARN SOME BEER MONEY. IT'LL BE A LAUGH. YOU COULD PLAY THE DRUMS.
DRUM TAPBOX
WASHBOARD
CONBELL
39/6
VICEROY
SKIFFLE
BOARD
FUN
FUN
FUN
IDEAL FOR PARTIES
Snare-and-cymbal
£10
Don't
miss
this!

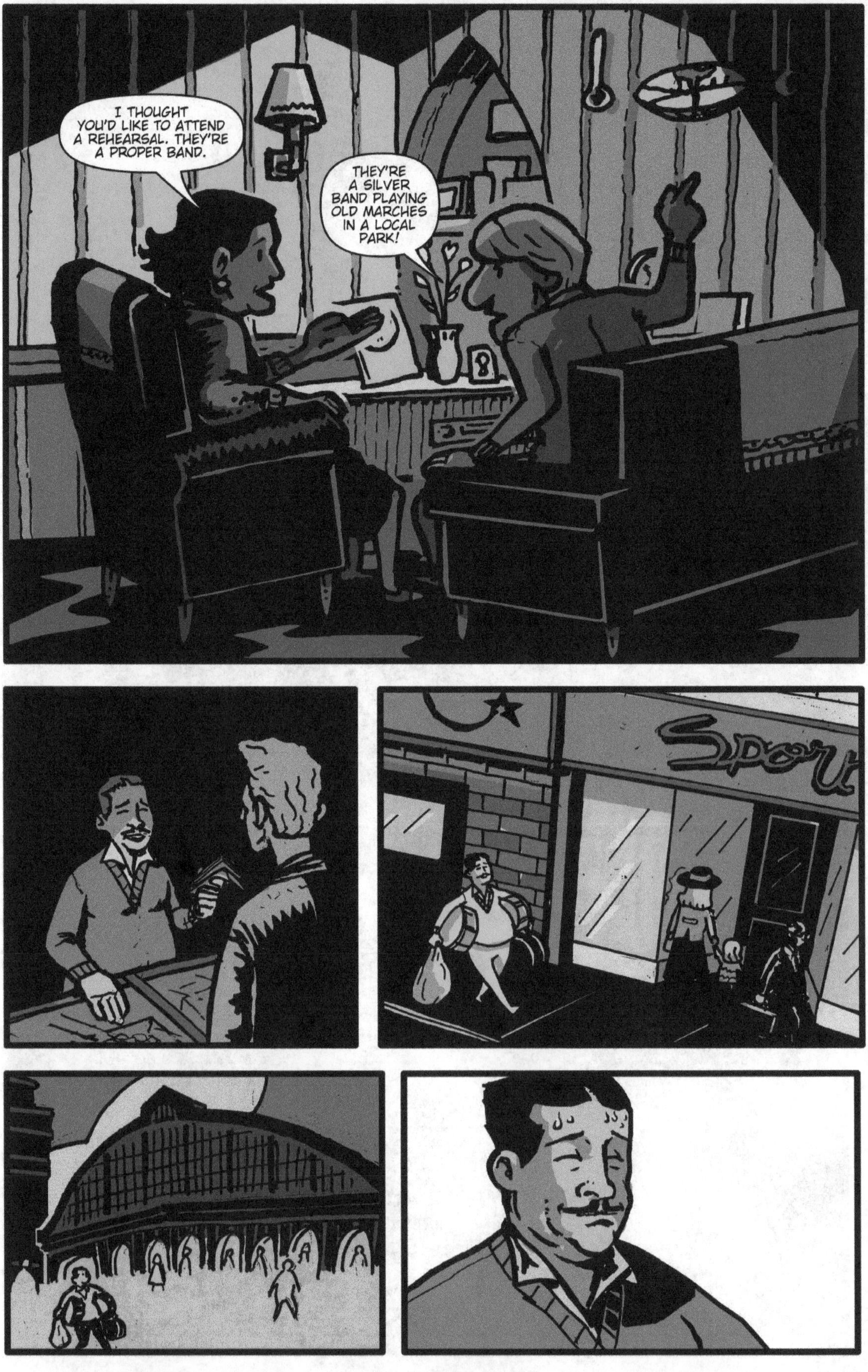
I THOUGHT YOU'D LIKE TO ATTEND A REHEARSAL. THEY'RE A PROPER BAND.
THEY'RE A SILVER BAND PLAYING OLD MARCHES IN A LOCAL PARK!

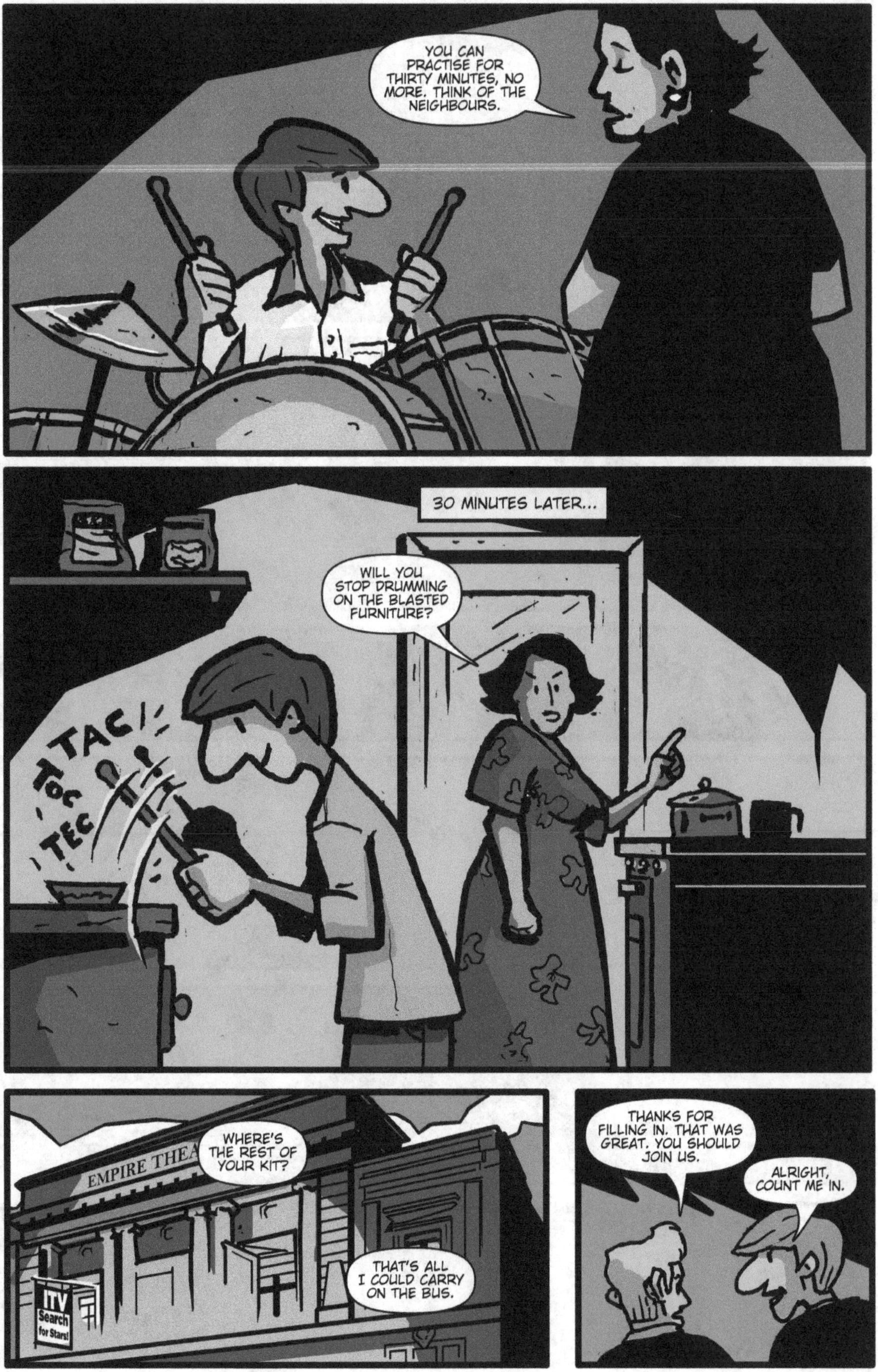
YOU CAN PRACTISE FOR THIRTY MINUTES, NO MORE. THINK OF THE NEIGHBOURS.
30 MINUTES LATER...
WILL YOU STOP DRUMMING ON THE BLASTED FURNITURE?
TAC
TOC
TEC
EMPIRE THEA
ITV Search for Stars!
WHERE'S THE REST OF YOUR KIT?
THAT'S ALL I COULD CARRY ON THE BUS.
THANKS FOR FILLING IN. THAT WAS GREAT. YOU SHOULD JOIN US.
ALRIGHT, COUNT ME IN.

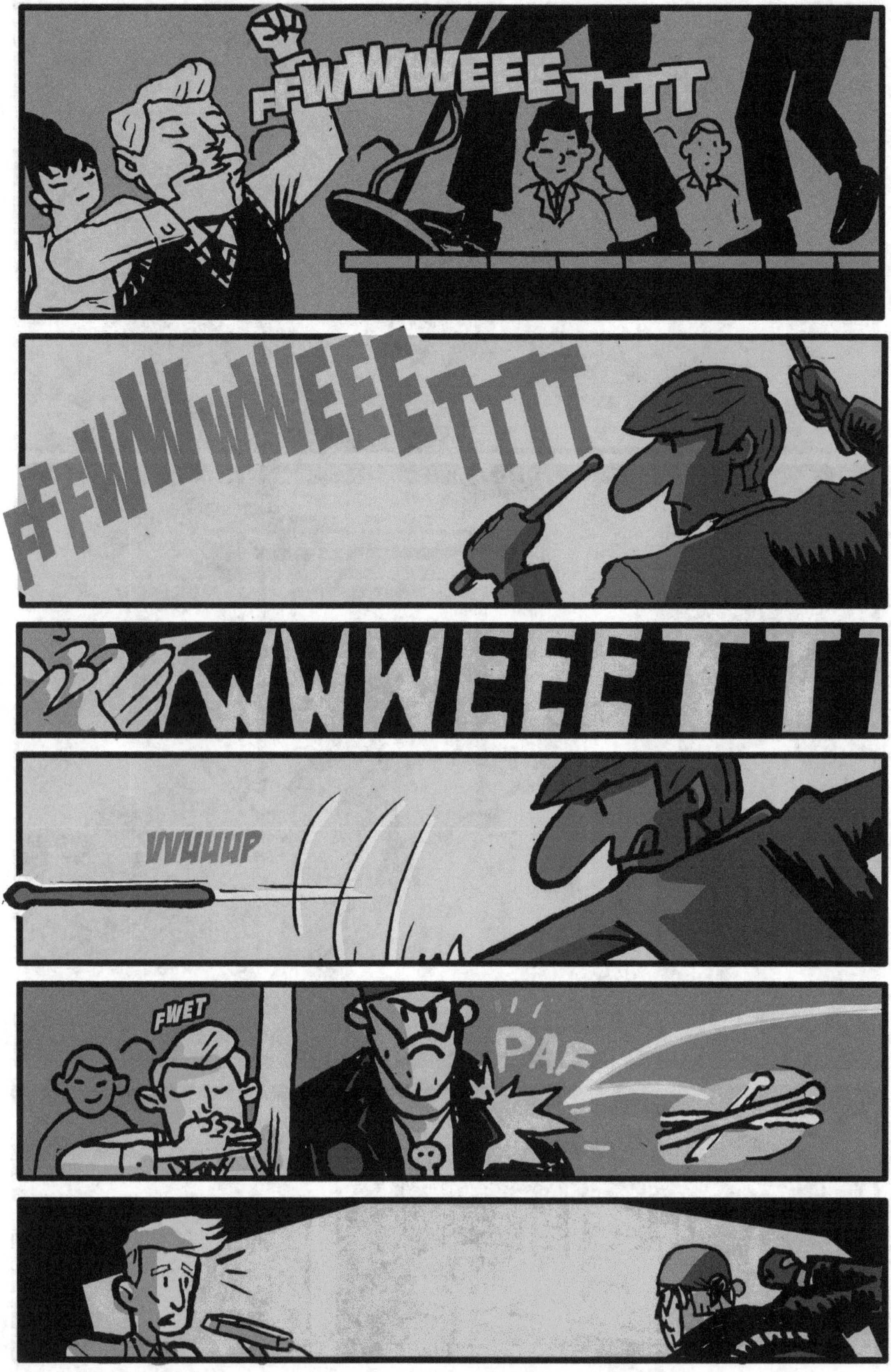

FFWWWEEETTTT
FFFWWWWWEEETTTT
WWWEEETTT
VVUUUP
FWET
PAF

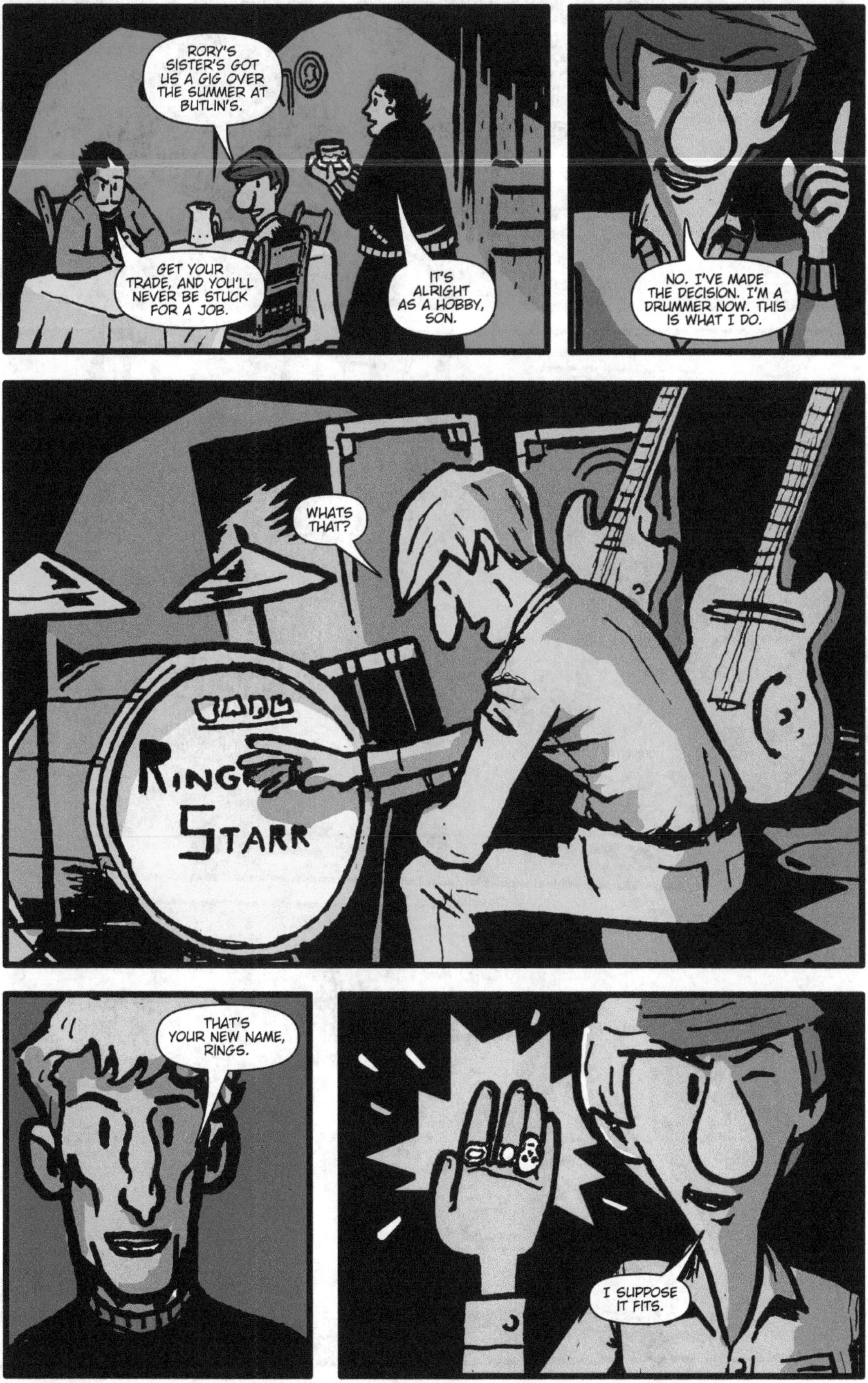
RORY'S SISTER'S GOT US A GIG OVER THE SUMMER AT BUTLIN'S.
GET YOUR TRADE, AND YOU'LL NEVER BE STUCK FOR A JOB.
IT'S ALRIGHT AS A HOBBY, SON.
NO. I'VE MADE THE DECISION. I'M A DRUMMER NOW. THIS IS WHAT I DO.
WHATS THAT?
RING
STARR
THAT'S YOUR NEW NAME, RINGS.
I SUPPOSE IT FITS.

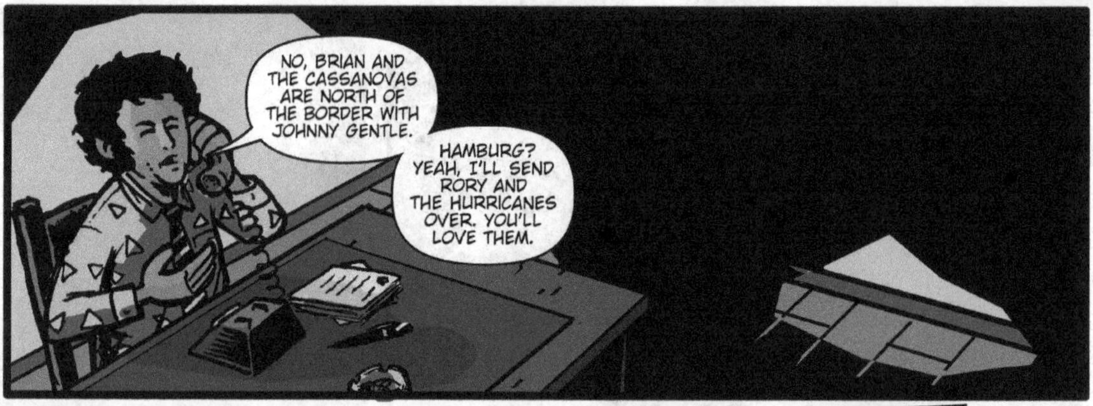
NO, BRIAN AND THE CASSANOVAS ARE NORTH OF THE BORDER WITH JOHNNY GENTLE.
HAMBURG? YEAH, I'LL SEND RORY AND THE HURRICANES OVER. YOU'LL LOVE THEM.

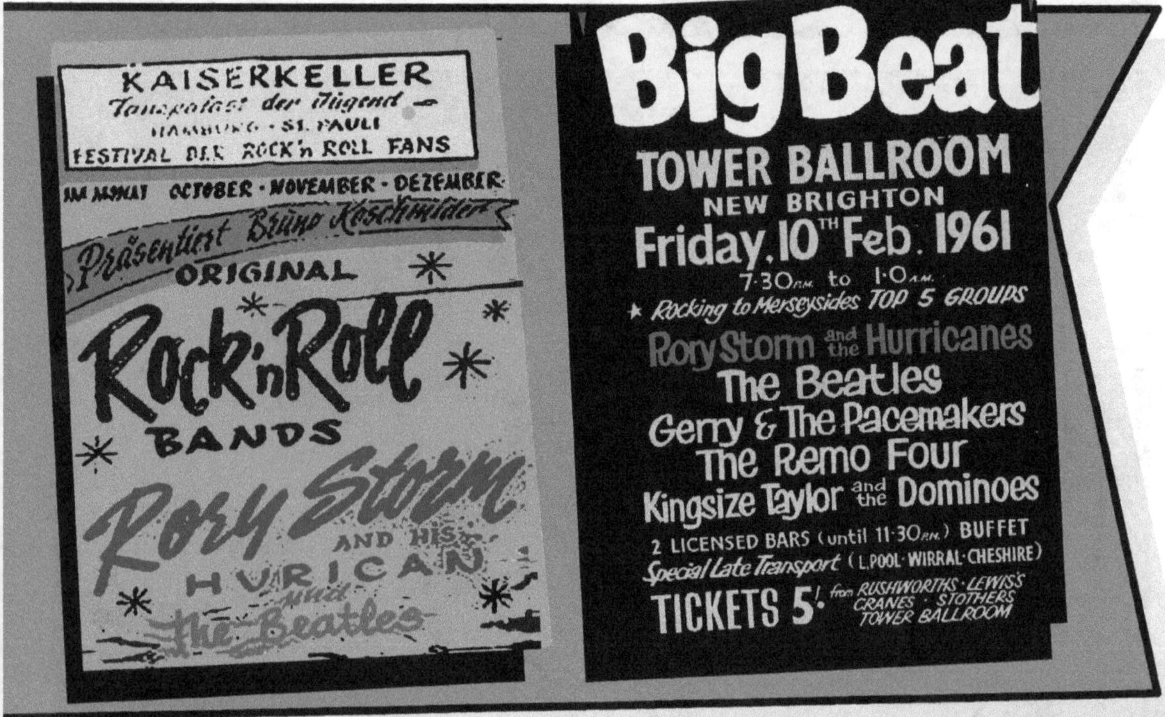
KAISERKELLER
ST. PAULI
FESTIVAL DER ROCK'n ROLL FANS
OCTOBER - NOVEMBER - DEZEMBER
Präsentiert Bruno Koschmider
ORIGINAL
Rock'n Roll
BANDS
Rory Storm
AND HIS
HURICAN
und
The Beatles
Big Beat
TOWER BALLROOM
NEW BRIGHTON
Friday, 10TH Feb. 1961
7·30 P.M. to 1·0 A.M.
★ Rocking to Merseysides TOP 5 GROUPS
Rory Storm and the Hurricanes
The Beatles
Gerry & The Pacemakers
The Remo Four
Kingsize Taylor and the Dominoes
2 LICENSED BARS (until 11·30 P.M.) BUFFET
Special Late Transport (L'POOL · WIRRAL · CHESHIRE)
TICKETS 5/- from RUSHWORTHS · LEWIS'S · CRANES · STOTHERS · TOWER BALLROOM

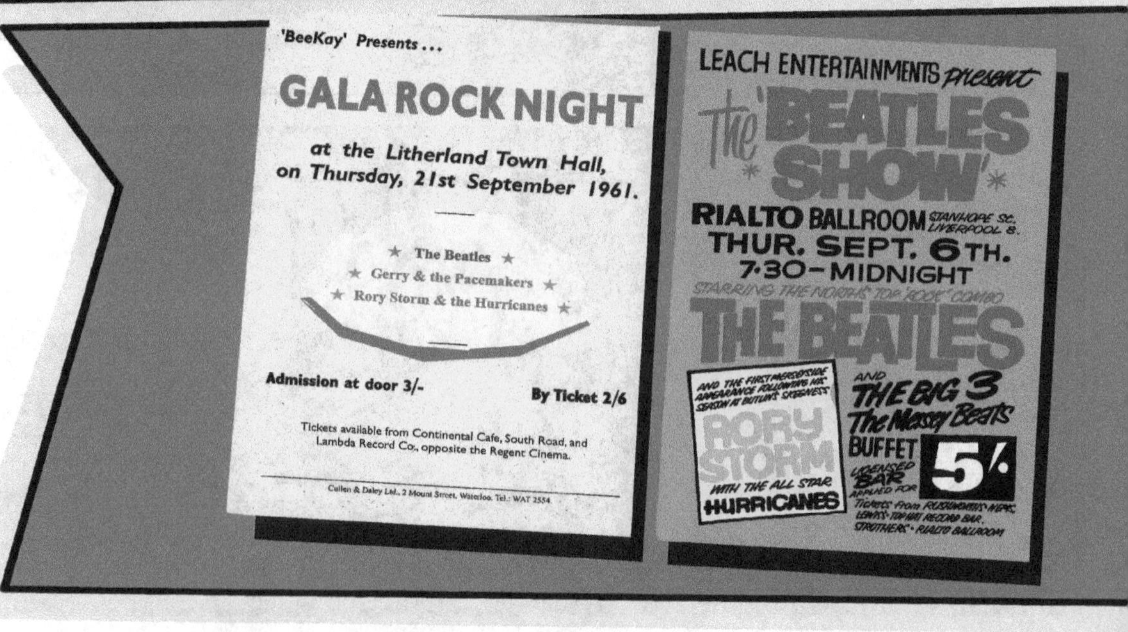
'BeeKay' Presents . . .
GALA ROCK NIGHT
at the Litherland Town Hall, on Thursday, 21st September 1961.
★ The Beatles ★
★ Gerry & the Pacemakers ★
★ Rory Storm & the Hurricanes ★
Admission at door 3/-
By Ticket 2/6
Tickets available from Continental Cafe, South Road, and Lambda Record Co., opposite the Regent Cinema.
Cullen & Daley Ltd., 2 Mount Street, Waterloo. Tel.: WAT 2554
LEACH ENTERTAINMENTS present
the 'BEATLES SHOW'
RIALTO BALLROOM STANHOPE St. LIVERPOOL 8.
THUR. SEPT. 6TH.
7·30 - MIDNIGHT
STARRING THE NORTH'S TOP 'ROCK' COMBO
THE BEATLES
AND THE FIRST MERSEYSIDE APPEARANCE FOLLOWING HIS SEASON AT BUTLIN'S SKEGNESS
RORY STORM
WITH THE ALL STAR HURRICANES
AND
THE BIG 3
The Mersey Beats
BUFFET
LICENSED BAR APPLIED FOR
5/-
STROTHERS · RIALTO BALLROOM

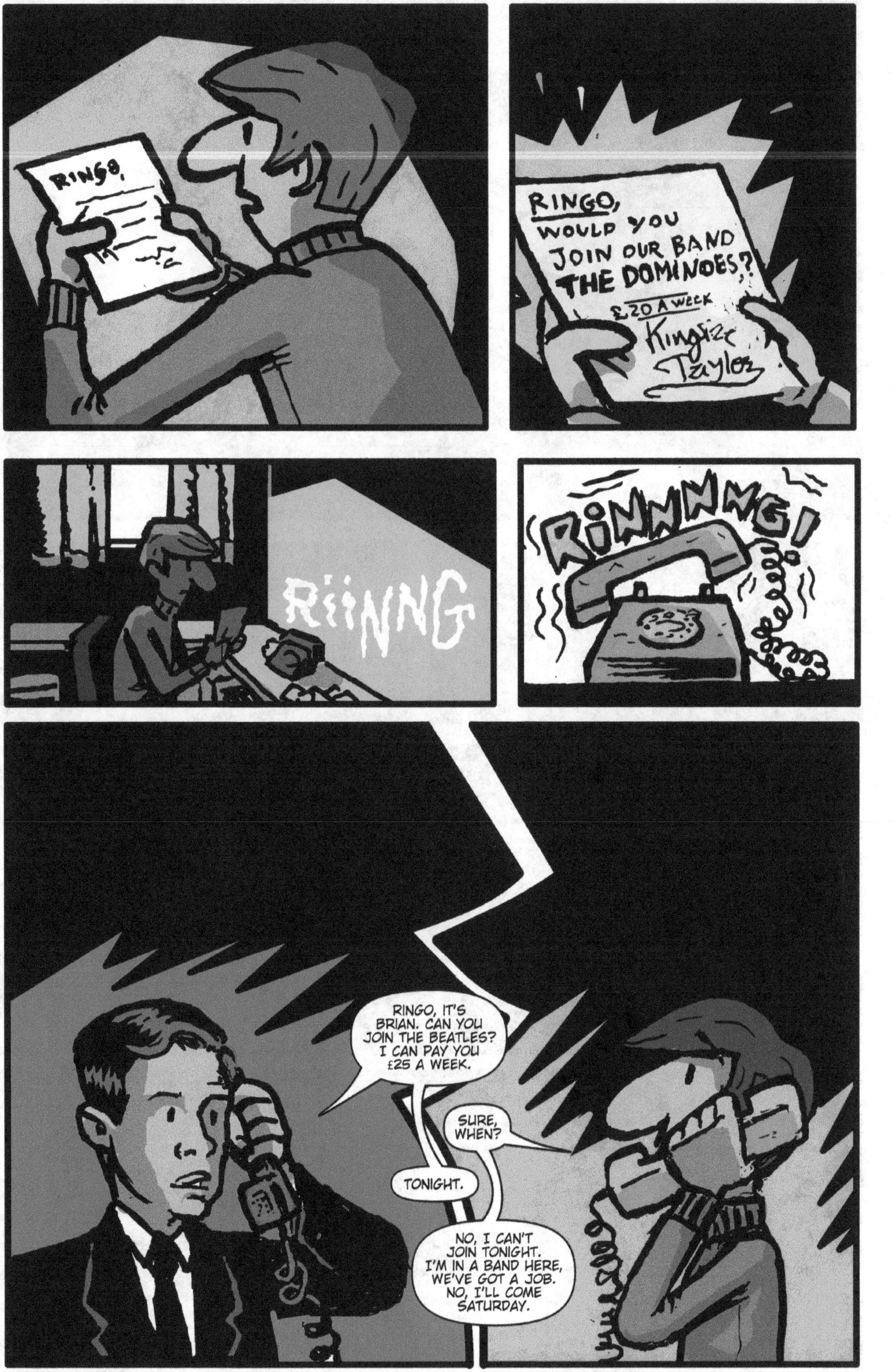
RINGO,
RINGO, WOULD YOU JOIN OUR BAND THE DOMINOES?
£20 A WEEK
Kingsize Taylor
RIINNG
RINNNNG!
RINGO, IT'S BRIAN. CAN YOU JOIN THE BEATLES? I CAN PAY YOU £25 A WEEK.
SURE, WHEN?
TONIGHT.
NO, I CAN'T JOIN TONIGHT. I'M IN A BAND HERE, WE'VE GOT A JOB. NO, I'LL COME SATURDAY.

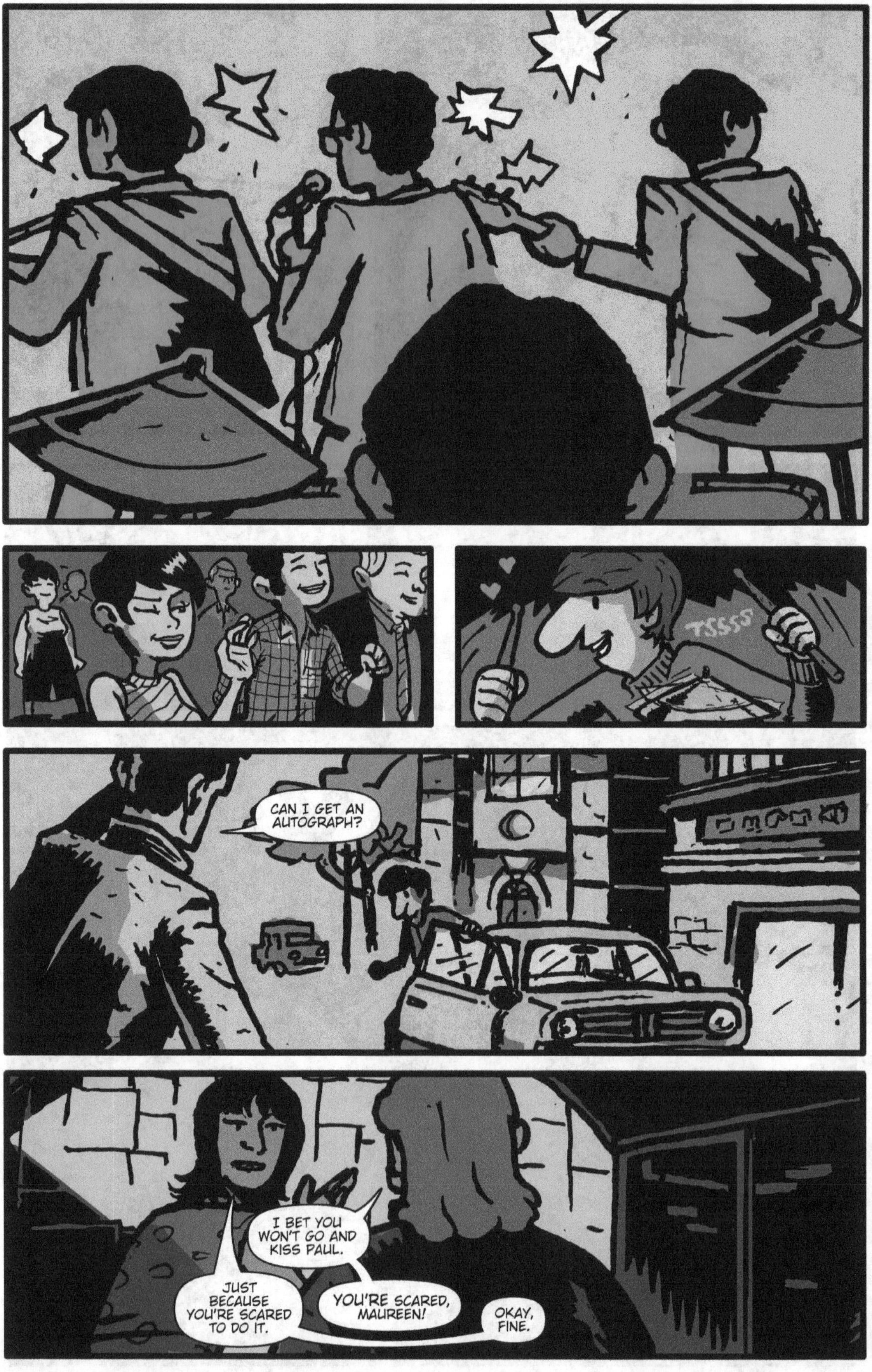
TSSSS
CAN I GET AN AUTOGRAPH?
I BET YOU WON'T GO AND KISS PAUL.
JUST BECAUSE YOU'RE SCARED TO DO IT.
YOU'RE SCARED, MAUREEN!
OKAY, FINE.

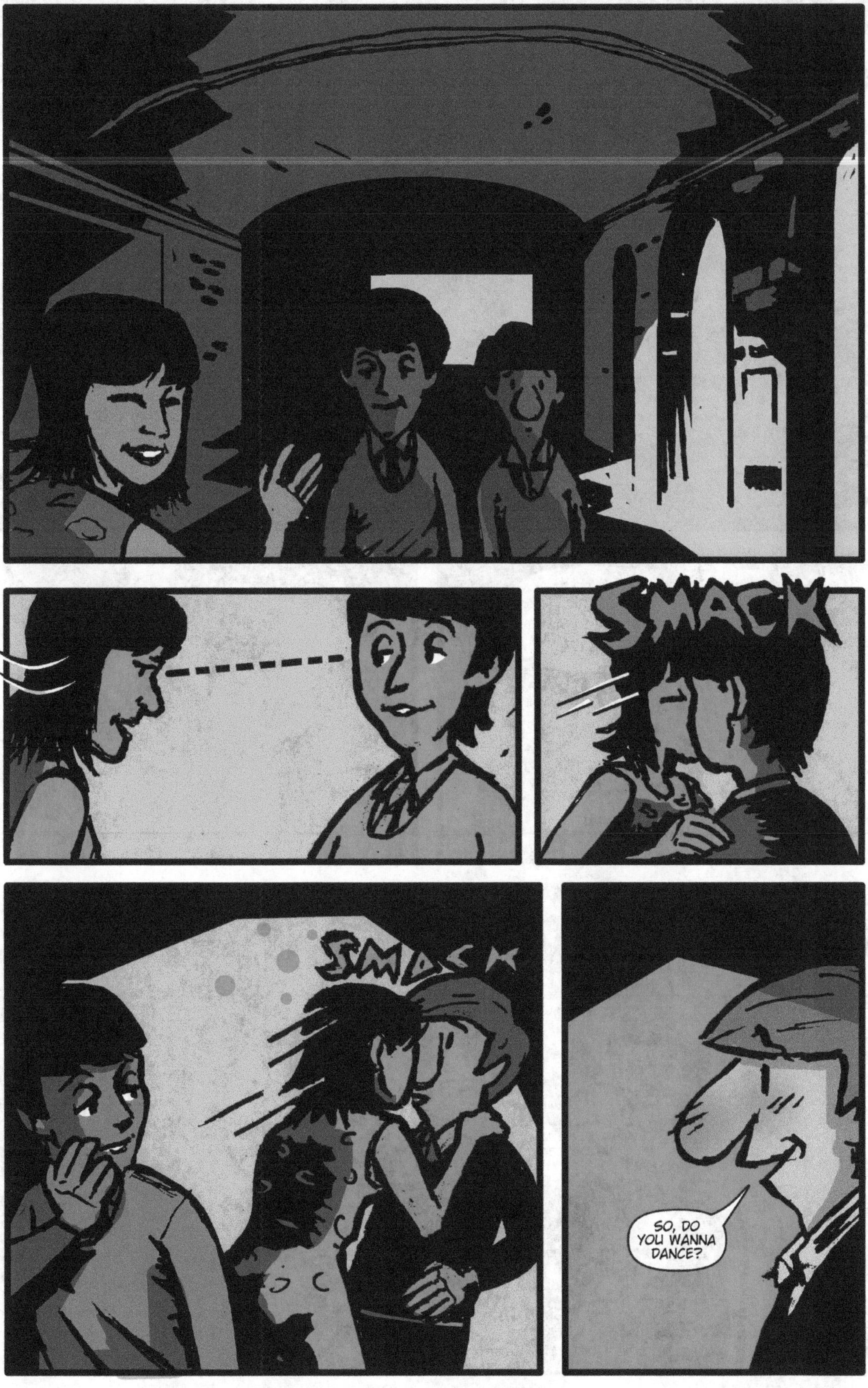
SMACK
SMACK
SO, DO YOU WANNA DANCE?

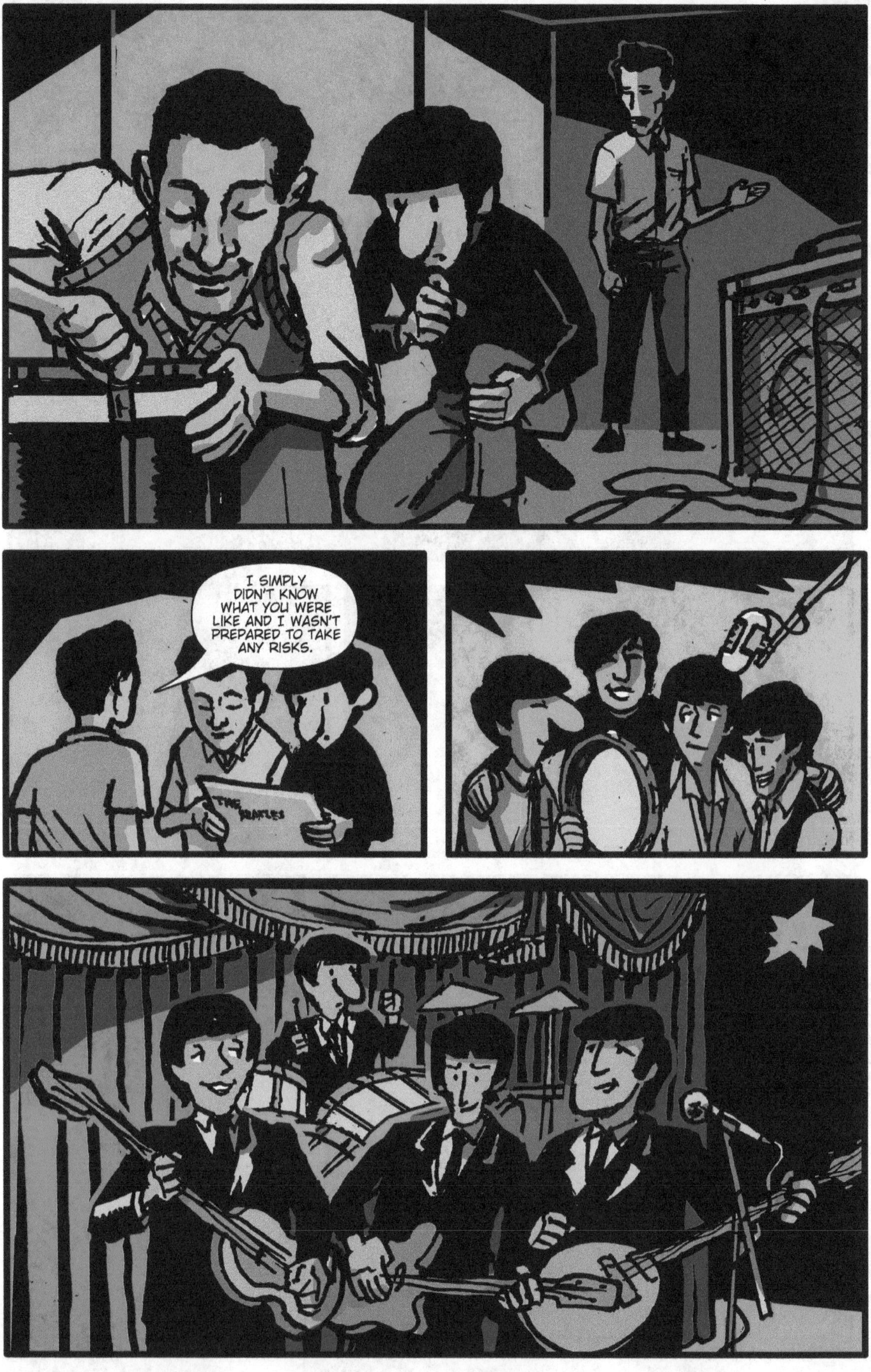
I SIMPLY DIDN'T KNOW WHAT YOU WERE LIKE AND I WASN'T PREPARED TO TAKE ANY RISKS.
THE BEATLES

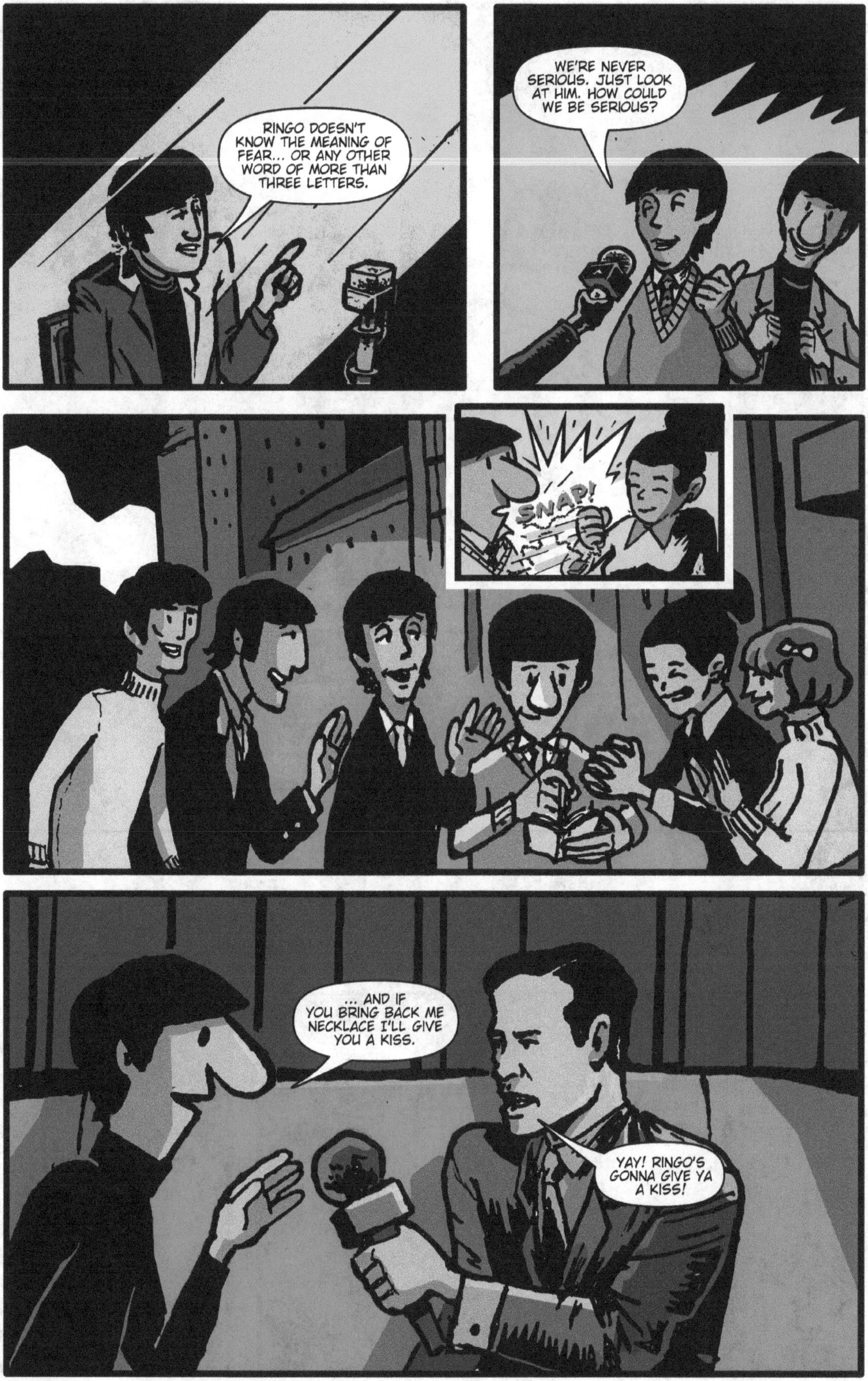
RINGO DOESN'T KNOW THE MEANING OF FEAR... OR ANY OTHER WORD OF MORE THAN THREE LETTERS.
WE'RE NEVER SERIOUS. JUST LOOK AT HIM. HOW COULD WE BE SERIOUS?
SNAP!
... AND IF YOU BRING BACK ME NECKLACE I'LL GIVE YOU A KISS.
YAY! RINGO'S GONNA GIVE YA A KISS!

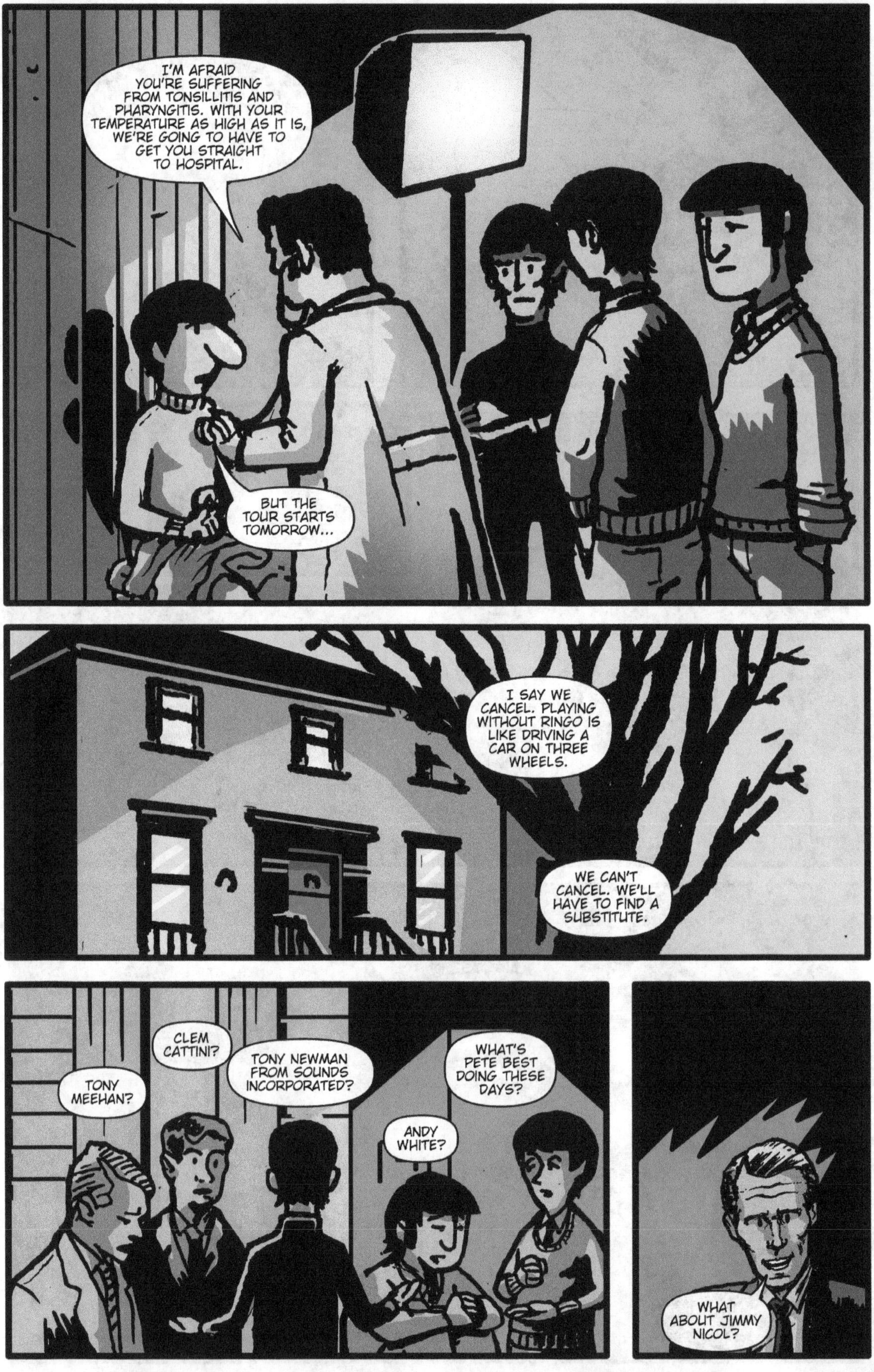
I'M AFRAID YOU'RE SUFFERING FROM TONSILLITIS AND PHARYNGITIS. WITH YOUR TEMPERATURE AS HIGH AS IT IS, WE'RE GOING TO HAVE TO GET YOU STRAIGHT TO HOSPITAL.
BUT THE TOUR STARTS TOMORROW...
I SAY WE CANCEL. PLAYING WITHOUT RINGO IS LIKE DRIVING A CAR ON THREE WHEELS.
WE CAN'T CANCEL. WE'LL HAVE TO FIND A SUBSTITUTE.
TONY MEEHAN?
CLEM CATTINI?
TONY NEWMAN FROM SOUNDS INCORPORATED?
WHAT'S PETE BEST DOING THESE DAYS?
ANDY WHITE?
WHAT ABOUT JIMMY NICOL?

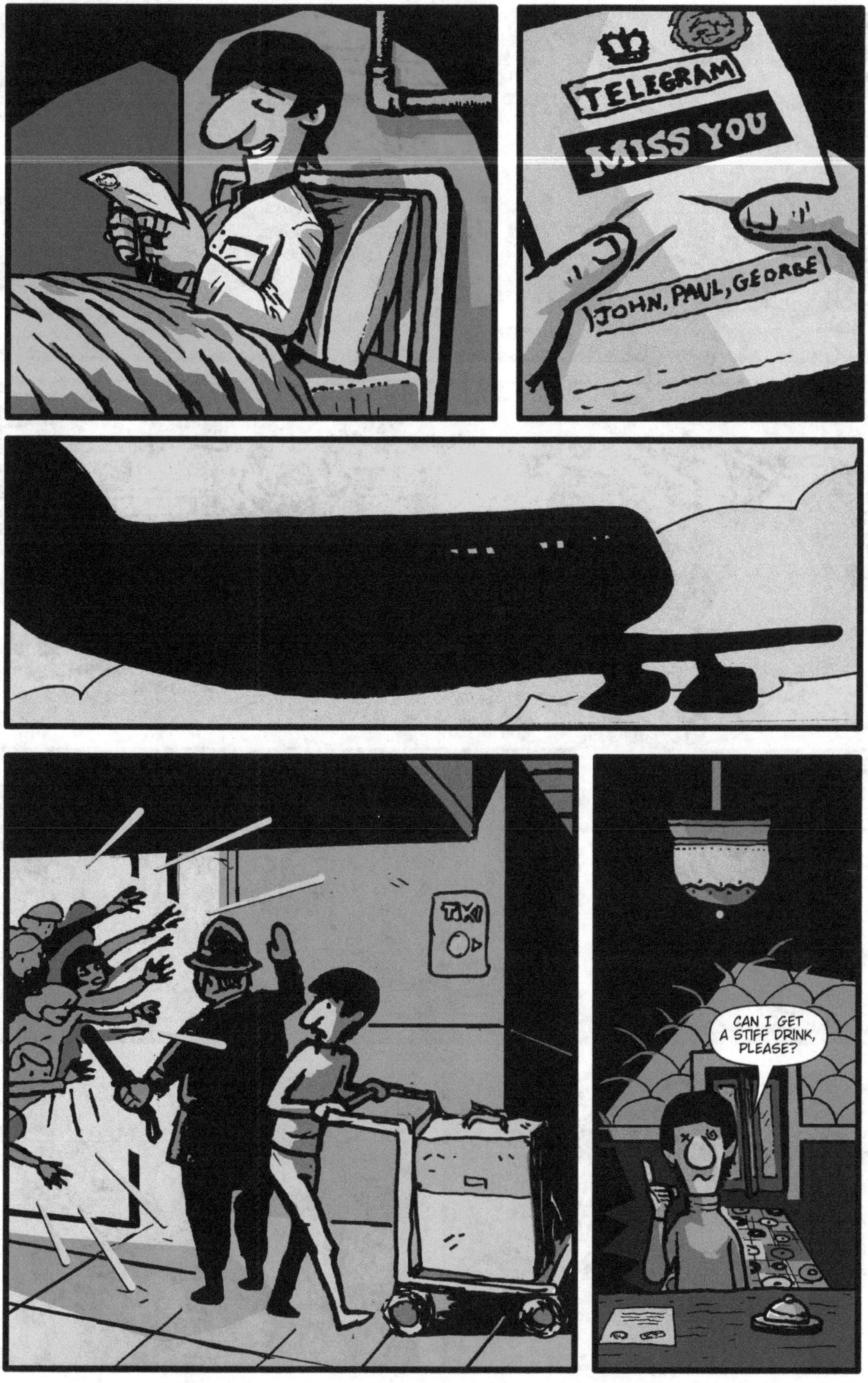
TELEGRAM
MISS YOU
JOHN, PAUL, GEORGE
TAXI
CAN I GET A STIFF DRINK, PLEASE?

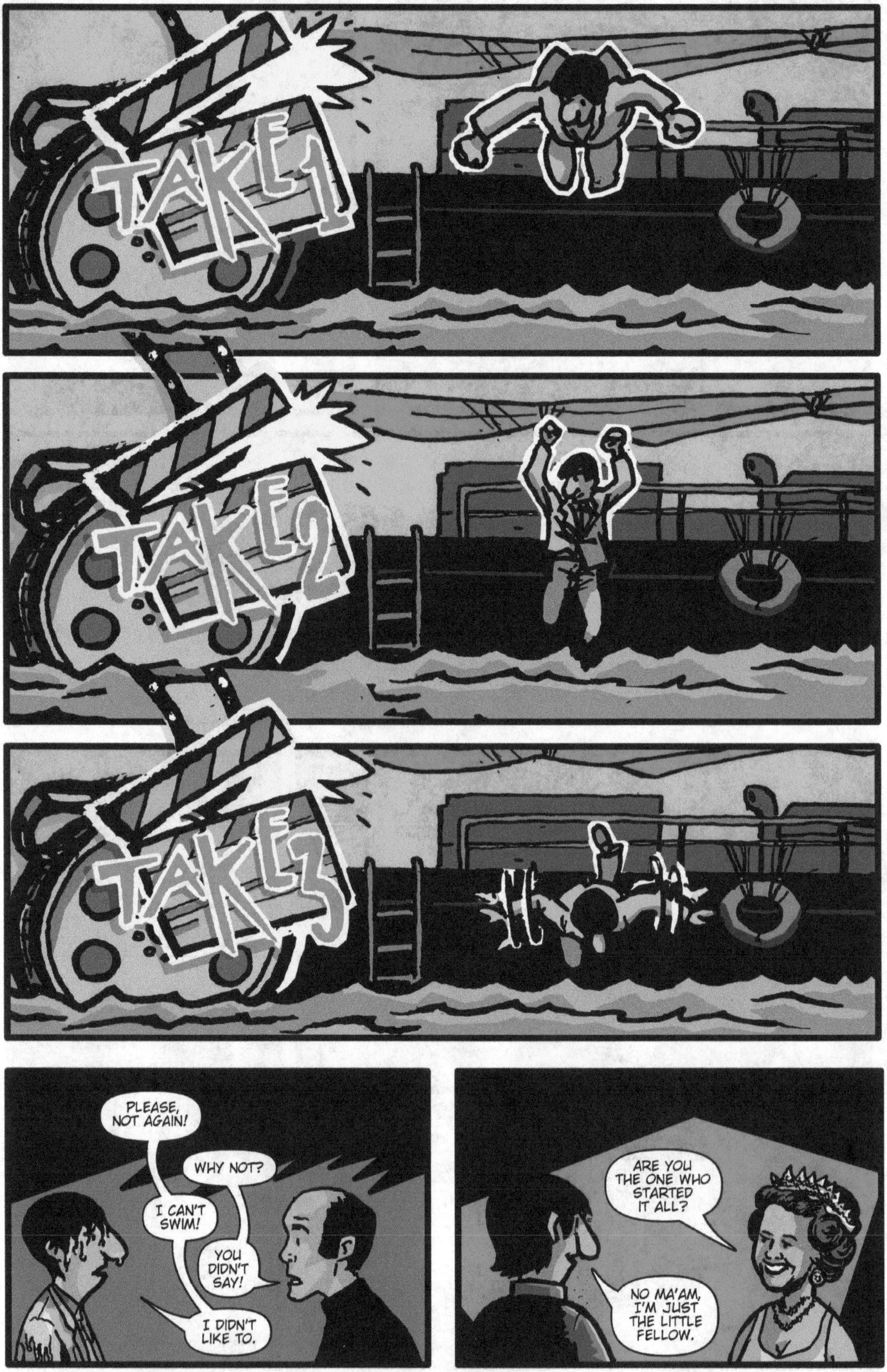
TAKE 1
TAKE 2
TAKE 3
PLEASE, NOT AGAIN!
WHY NOT?
I CAN'T SWIM!
YOU DIDN'T SAY!
I DIDN'T LIKE TO.
ARE YOU THE ONE WHO STARTED IT ALL?
NO MA'AM, I'M JUST THE LITTLE FELLOW.

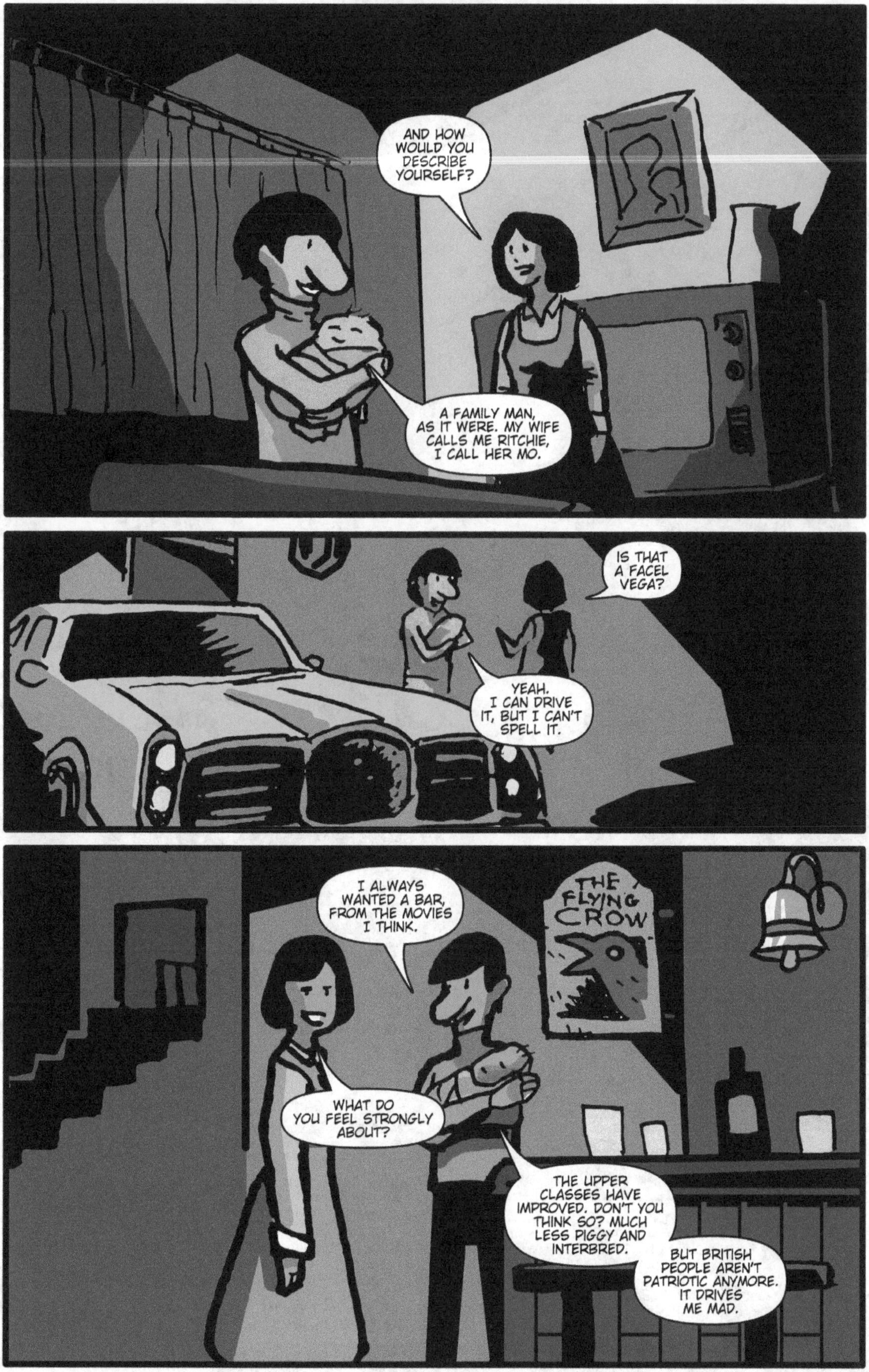
AND HOW WOULD YOU DESCRIBE YOURSELF?
A FAMILY MAN, AS IT WERE. MY WIFE CALLS ME RITCHIE, I CALL HER MO.
IS THAT A FACEL VEGA?
YEAH. I CAN DRIVE IT, BUT I CAN'T SPELL IT.
I ALWAYS WANTED A BAR, FROM THE MOVIES I THINK.
THE FLYING CROW
WHAT DO YOU FEEL STRONGLY ABOUT?
THE UPPER CLASSES HAVE IMPROVED. DON'T YOU THINK SO? MUCH LESS PIGGY AND INTERBRED.
BUT BRITISH PEOPLE AREN'T PATRIOTIC ANYMORE. IT DRIVES ME MAD.

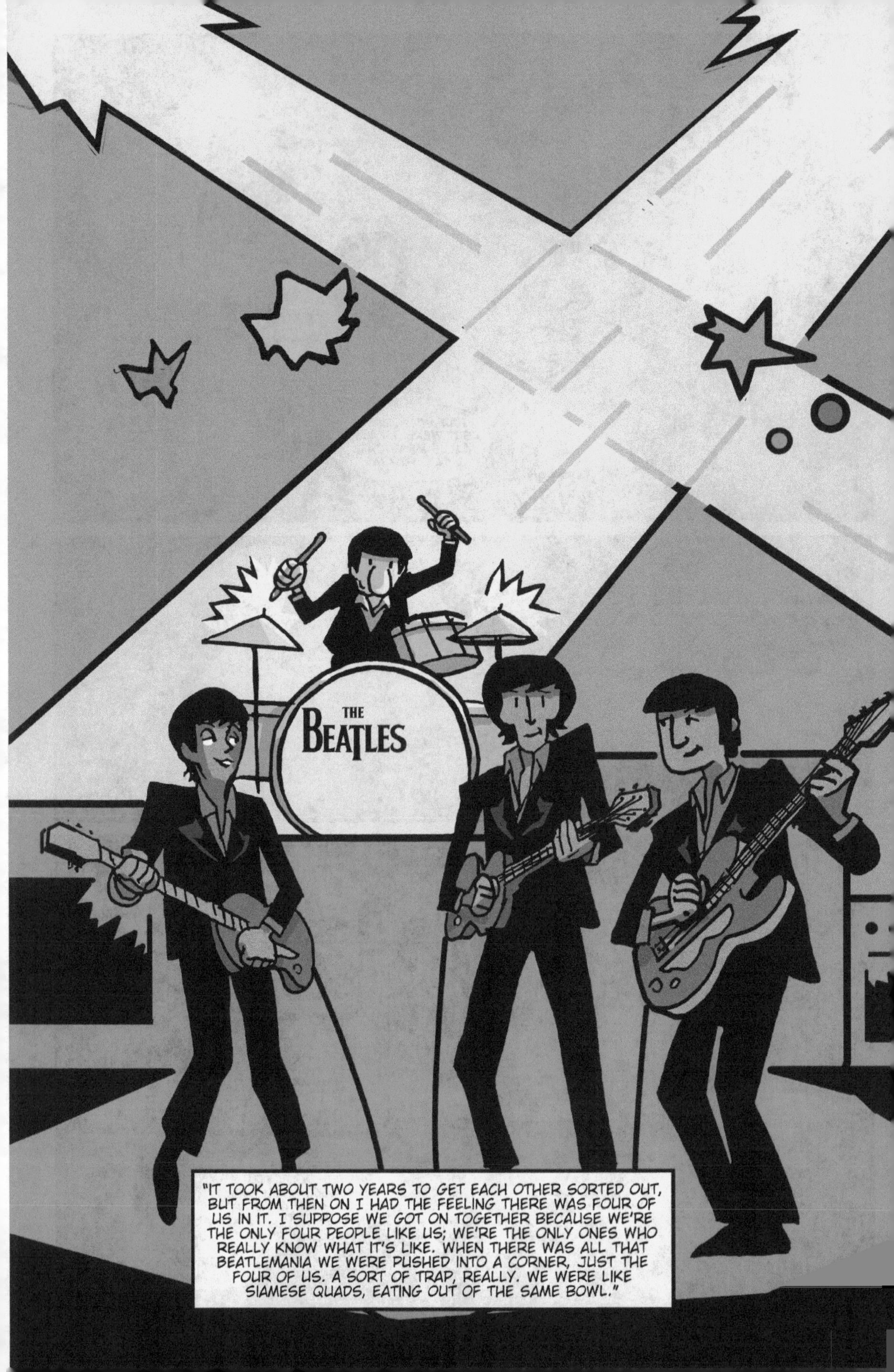
THE BEATLES
"IT TOOK ABOUT TWO YEARS TO GET EACH OTHER SORTED OUT, BUT FROM THEN ON I HAD THE FEELING THERE WAS FOUR OF US IN IT. I SUPPOSE WE GOT ON TOGETHER BECAUSE WE'RE THE ONLY FOUR PEOPLE LIKE US; WE'RE THE ONLY ONES WHO REALLY KNOW WHAT IT'S LIKE. WHEN THERE WAS ALL THAT BEATLEMANIA WE WERE PUSHED INTO A CORNER, JUST THE FOUR OF US. A SORT OF TRAP, REALLY. WE WERE LIKE SIAMESE QUADS, EATING OUT OF THE SAME BOWL."

David Cromarty — Writer

Victor Moura — Pencils

Benjamin Glibert — Letters

Victor Moura — Colors

Graham Hill — Cover

Darren G. Davis
Publisher

Maggie Jessup
Publicity

Susan Ferris
Entertainment Manager

Steven Diggs Jr.
Marketing Manager

ORBIT AND CONTENTS ARE COPYRIGHT © AND ™ DARREN G. DAVIS. ALL RIGHTS RESERVED. TIDALWAVE IS COPYRIGHT © AND ™ DARREN G. DAVIS. ALL RIGHTS RESERVED. ANY REPRODUCTION OF THIS MATERIAL IS STRICTLY PROHIBITED IN ANY MEDIA FORM OTHER THAN FOR PROMOTIONAL PURPOSES UNLESS DARREN G. DAVIS OR TIDALWAVE PUBLISHING GIVES WRITTEN CONSENT. PRINTED IN THE USA
www.tidalwavecomics.com

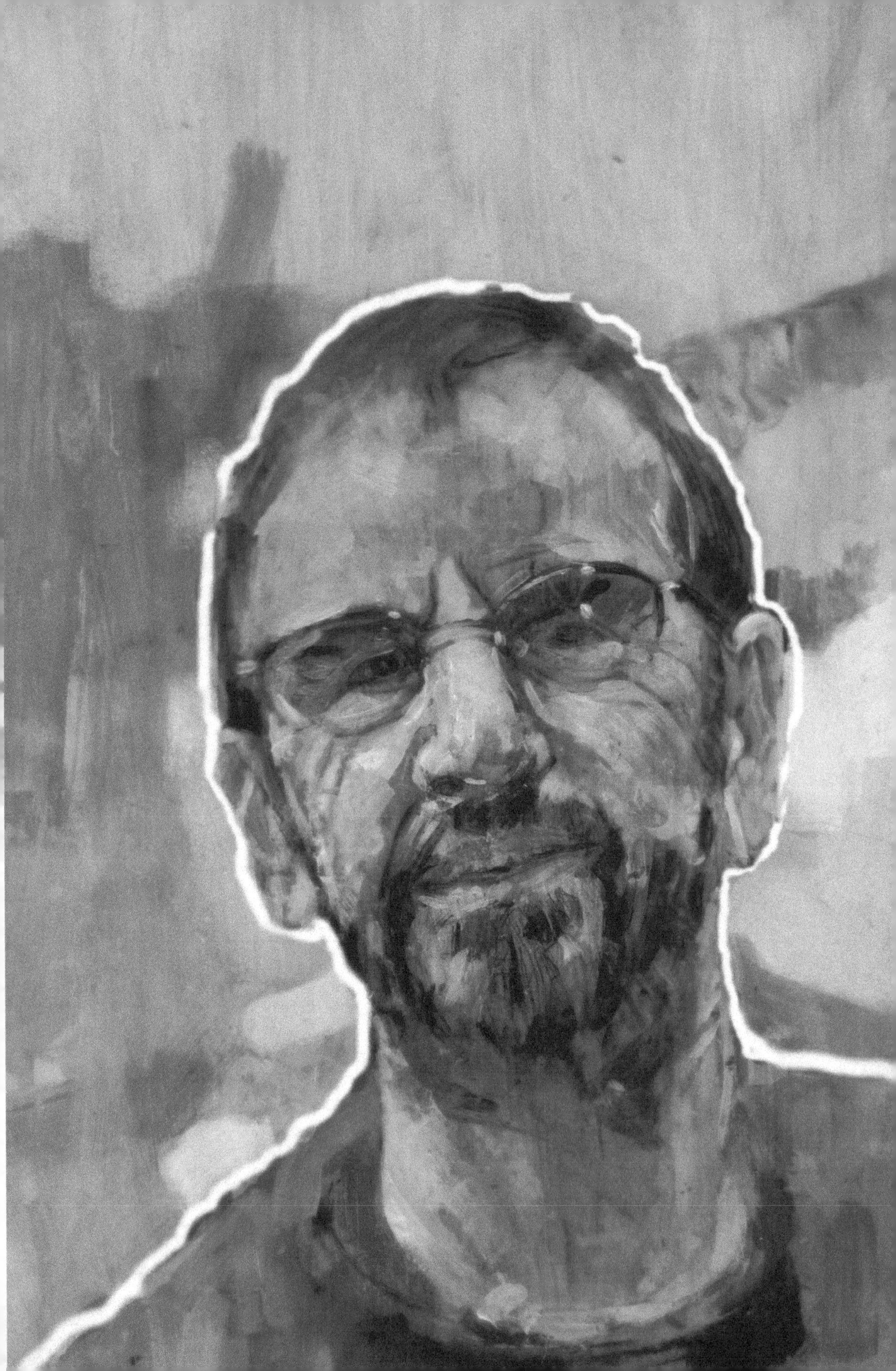

CPSIA information can be obtained
at www.ICGtesting.com
Printed in the USA
BVHW011419110122
625980BV00008B/205